Bird Watching: What You Need To Know About Birds

The Important Things to Bird Watching Mastery

By: Michael Miller

9781634289986

Publishers Notes

Disclaimer – Speedy Publishing LLC

This publication is intended to provide helpful and informative material. It is not intended to diagnose, treat, cure, or prevent any health problem or condition, nor is intended to replace the advice of a physician. No action should be taken solely on the contents of this book. Always consult your physician or qualified health-care professional on any matters regarding your health and before adopting any suggestions in this book or drawing inferences from it.

The author and publisher specifically disclaim all responsibility for any liability, loss or risk, personal or otherwise, which is incurred as a consequence, directly or indirectly, from the use or application of any contents of this book.

Any and all product names referenced within this book are the trademarks of their respective owners. None of these owners have sponsored, authorized, endorsed, or approved this book.

Always read all information provided by the manufacturers' product labels before using their products. The author and publisher are not responsible for claims made by manufacturers.

This book was originally printed before 2014. This is an adapted reprint by Speedy Publishing LLC with newly updated content designed to help readers with much more accurate and timely information and data.

Speedy Publishing LLC

40 E Main Street, Newark, Delaware, 19711

Contact Us: 1-888-248-4521

Website: http://www.speedypublishing.co

REPRINTED Paperback Edition: ISBN: 9781634289986

Manufactured in the United States of America

DEDICATION

I dedicate this book to all who are bird watching enthusiasts and to those who are nature lovers who want to venture into bird watching. This book will give you detail information to master bird watching.

Table of Contents

Publishers Notes 2

Dedication 3

Table of Contents 4

Chapter 1- Introduction to Bird Watching Mastery 5

Chapter 2- Things Needed for Bird Watching 11

Chapter 3- Where to Bird Watching? 28

Chapter 4- Bird Watching Mastery with Your Ears 40

Chapter 5- Bird Watching Mastery and Bird Houses 50

Chapter 6- Know the Prominent Contributors and Organization to Bird Watching 59

Chapter 7- Important Behavior Observation During Bird Watching 66

Chapter 8- The Effects of Bird Watching to the Environment 71

About The Author 78

Chapter 1 - Introduction to Bird Watching Mastery

Imagine yourself lying in your bed. The morning sun is just peeking through your window. Along with the sun, you hear the melodious song of birds chirping their "good mornings" to each other -- and to you! Have you ever wondered what those birds looked like? Why they are close enough for you to hear? What interesting characteristics they have about them?

Bird watching is a sport that has been around for years. In fact, today, bird watching is the second fastest growing hobby in America, bested only by gardening. A whole new language has emerged along with it. Those in the know also refer to bird watching simply as "birding" and the people who do it as "birders".

People of all ages enjoy seeking out the birds of their region, watching them in their natural habitat, and enjoying the songs they have to offer. Birds can be fascinating creatures with much to offer

Bird Watching Mastery: What You Need To Know About Birds
those who care to study their lives. Much can be learned from where they roost, how they fly, and what they sing. We can even go so far as to say that watching birds can reveal things about nature and the beauty that exists in nature.

"I once had a sparrow alight upon my shoulder for a moment, while I was hoeing in a village garden, and I felt that I was more distinguished by that circumstance that I should have been by any epaulet I could have worn."

~Henry David Thoreau

Birding can be done anywhere. You can find all kinds of species in your local park, any forest, and even in your own backyard!

No one knows the sights and sounds of nature quite like a bird watcher. By taking a half-second look at a small darting assemblage of black, yellow, and white feathers and adding a musical note that sounds something like "chirp", a birder can tell you, not only the general species of that bird, but he or she can narrow it down to the exact bird.

To distinguish among the 900+ species of birds found in the U.S., birders must quickly process a great deal of information on color patterns, call notes, and even the shapes of bills. They have to know what to key in on when they see a strange bird, noting its overall shape, how it moves through a bush or tree, and the shape of its wings. Such sensory work-outs help to develop great visual and hearing acuity among birders. In fact, birders are generally much more observant than the average person.

To the beginning bird watcher, this might seem like an unbelievable task that they might never be able to achieve. Trying to identify even common species can be extremely frustrating, and many people give up before they ever actually begin.

Finding birds and identifying them can happen in an instance. A small black bird flashes up to the top of a bush. You grab your binoculars and start flipping through your field guide. You take another look at the bird, flip back a page or two... suddenly the bird is gone, but there is a different one lower in the bush. All that page riffling and binocular lifting begins anew.

Birding can make you more familiar with the natural beauty of the world and perhaps will lead you to appreciate how quickly that beauty is being lost. Birding can coax you into new country and enables you to take in all the fresh air and impressive scenery that you can hold. Most important, though, is the fact that birding is simply too much fun to be missed.

The type of information presented here is second nature to an experienced birder, but it can take many months of hard toil for the beginning bird watcher to grasp these concepts and techniques. Even with the information spelled out here, you still have to supply a good bit of patience and sweat to become one of the truly tuned-in nature watchers.

We have tried to strip away some of the mystique of Bird watching and expose the bare essentials, but practice and patience are just as important to Bird watching as they are to sports, music, and other recreational activities. You can't expect to record 150 different species on your first outing (though this will be possible later on) or to identify all those confusing birds. You'll have to work at it.

This book is intended to help you get beyond the frustrating early stage. It's a crash course in the basics of bird watching or "birding".

Bird Watching Mastery: What You Need To Know About Birds

Hopefully, with the guidance of this book, you'll be well on your way to greater enjoyment of the world around you since birding focuses on some of the most spectacular creatures on earth.

Birds are highly visual creatures - just like people - and some species wear breathtaking combinations of yellows, blues, reds, blacks, and greens to making them more obvious to the naked eye. They also come in a wide variety of shapes and forms, which adds considerably to the pleasures of Bird watching.

You just might find that bird watching isn't only fun, it's a learning experience as well! Birding gets you outdoors, give you exercise makes you think, and hone your observational skills. Read on and join us as we look at bird watching for beginners!

WHY WATCH BIRDS?

Birds have long delighted people all over the world because of their beauty and their power of flight. Birds are everywhere, and everywhere they are different. Birds are mysterious, beautiful, and sometimes wonderfully elusive.

Historically, they used to be considered omens. The ancient Romans believed that the flights and calls of birds could foretell the future.

Today, modern science still uses birds as a kind of oracle. Changes in bird populations can reflect the health of the environment.

Birding also fulfills another basic instinct—the quest for knowledge. Birding is about acquiring knowledge. Not just about birds' names, but also about their songs, their behavior, and how they relate to the rest of nature. It's a perfect opportunity to enjoy a unique human pleasure—the successful exercise of lore.

In fact, amateur birders often get to make real contributions to scientific knowledge. Today, much of what ornithology knows about birds has come from the observations of ordinary but dedicated birders.

Some birds are indicator species, like the USA's national bird, the bald eagle. They forecast environmental conditions. The knowledge of birds can help us plan a better, more sustainable relationship with nature.

Maybe we watch birds because they are accessible: wherever we go, birds are there, usually active while we are active, sleeping while we sleep. In our own backyards, we lure them with birdfeeders and birdhouses, and by placing shrubs, water, and appropriate plants in the landscape. More than any creature except perhaps insects, birds visibly share our outdoor space, and if we have to travel miles and sit quietly for patient hours in order to see a rare or elusive bird, that makes it a treasure hunt.

We love treasure hunts and we love novelty. Birds provide both. While many birds have very wide ranges, the birds of one country tend to differ from the birds of another; even if you find the birds at home rather ordinary, you will be thrilled by unfamiliar birds when you travel. You will see the same type of bird in varied locations, but the birds will be different.

Birds are beautiful. Their brilliant hues offer a companion to their color vision. Birds flash past in every shade from emerald to vermillion, beautiful as showy flower blossoms but usually more surprising. An endless variety of patterns, shapes, and sizes delight us. Even the common crow has a lovely sheen and certain elegance. Yes, birds are an awesome part of life – how could we not watch birds?

Bird Watching Mastery: What You Need To Know About Birds

Bird watching is FUN! It gives you a great excuse to leave your television behind and venture out into the elements. Need a good reason to head out and go for a walk? Bring along your binoculars. It provides a healthy activity that just about anyone can enjoy. You don't need good knees like skiing. You don't even need to be able to venture beyond your own back yard. Bird feeders placed on window sills allow individuals with limited to enjoy birds with little or no effort.

Birding is also the ideal solitary sport. There's a special pleasure in going out alone to bird. Your mind settles down. Your senses open up, and all nature seems to become your friend. Birding is a sport of many moods, and it serves the causes of companionship and solitude equally well.

Be warned, however, Birding can be addictive. You may find yourself obsessed with some rare species that may have been reported locally. You find yourself getting up earlier and earlier to put in a few hours of birding before work. You begin looking at your landscaping in a whole new way as you start planting more bird friendly plants, installing feeders and bird baths and reducing the use of harmful chemicals.

As we've said, birds can be fascinating creatures. If you've never watched them before, just try for a few moments in the early morning light. Look at how they soar through the air. Listen to their morning songs. You can find great peace and great enlightenment in birds. How would you be able to truly enjoy these creatures unless you watched them? It's time to get started in bird watching!

Chapter 2- Things Needed for Bird Watching

The best part about bird watching is that you don't need much in the way of tools to do it effectively. You should just start with a good pair of binoculars, a field guide, a notebook, and a camera. Let's look at each component individually.

Binoculars

You need binoculars to better see the birds. You will soon discover an ironic fact. The best birders have the best binoculars - even though they can identify a bird 100 yards away by its silhouette. Newcomers with a cheap binocular see a fuzzy ball of feathers and don't have a clue which bird it is. There is an unbelievable difference between a $59 binocular and a $900 binocular.

Bird Watching Mastery: What You Need To Know About Birds

Binoculars are a birder's eyes on the world, and they can greatly affect the quality of a bird outing. Good binoculars make for good birding, while bad binoculars can lead to missed birds and severe headaches induced by blurred images, double vision, and eye strain.

Binoculars come in many different shapes and forms and carry such descriptions as "roof prism," "close focus," "armor coated," etc. At the outset, you don't need to spend too much time deciphering this arcane lexicon. If you really get hooked on bird watching, you can learn more about binoculars later and trade in for a better pair. A decent pair of binoculars will run you around $60 depending on where you live.

There are a few simple rules to consider and questions to ask when purchasing your first pair of binoculars.

1. Make sure the power (or magnification) is at least 7-power. The power is the first number given in the numerical notation that describes binoculars. For example, a "7 X 35" pair of "glasses" will make objects appear as if they are seven times as close as they actually are. Seven-power binoculars are about the minimum needed to see birds well. Binoculars 10-power or stronger can be difficult for some birders to hold steady.

2. Make sure that the second number ("35" for a "7 X 35" pair of glasses) is at least five times as large as the power (e.g., "7 X 35," "8 X 40," etc.). This second number describes the diameter, in millimeters, of the large lens that faces the object of interest - the "objective" lens. The larger this lens is, the greater the amount of light the binoculars gather and thus the easier it will be to see characteristics in dim light or on a dull-colored bird.

3. Are the binoculars too heavy for you to carry and use for at least two hours straight? Don't end up with a hunchback because your binoculars act like a yoke.

4. Can you flex the barrels of the binoculars fairly easily? To test to see if they are too flexible, spread the barrels out as far as possible and then hold onto only one of the barrels. Does the free barrel slip or fall from the spread position? It shouldn't.

5. When held a foot away, do the large objective lenses reflect a bluish or purplish tinge? If they do, the lenses are color-coated. This coating reduces internal glare in the binoculars and increases the amount of light that actually comes to your eyes. Check lenses to make sure the coatings are free of any blotches or scrapes.

6. Can you bring the barrels of the binoculars close enough together so that the image you see merges into a single, clear image within a single, perfect circle? If the image isn't singular or clear, the binoculars may be out of alignment or the eyepieces may not come close enough together to accommodate your eyes. These two problems may lead to eye strain and severe headaches.

7. Do you wear prescription eyeglasses? If you do, your binoculars should have rubber eye cups that fold back. This allows you to put your eyeglasses up closer to the eyepieces of your binoculars and gives you a much larger field of view.

8. Do the binoculars produce a clear image of an object only 20 feet away? Some binoculars do not focus on objects this close, so you may miss the sparrow or warbler that skulks in a nearby bush.

9. Look at a sign with large lettering. Do the letters close to the edge of the field of view appear as precise and well-formed as the letters in the center of the field of view? Image distortion towards

Bird Watching Mastery: What You Need To Know About Birds

the edge of binoculars is common in bad binoculars - like looking through a fish-eye lens. Look for a pair that has minimal distortion

10. When you focus on a license plate or small sign two blocks away, are the letters and numbers clear? If they're not, choose a different pair!

A general list of "don'ts" to consider when buying binoculars:

• Don't buy compact or pocket-sized binoculars (typically 8 x 21, or 10 x 21) as your primary pair for birding. The size and weight are attractive, but no matter how good the optics, compacts provide a lower quality image than mid- or full-size binoculars. Another drawback is that most compacts have a narrow field of view, which makes it very difficult to locate and follow birds.

• Don't buy zoom binoculars. Expert birders report them as being inferior.

• Don't seek advice on buying optics from non-birders. Hikers, hunters, and boaters have different needs than birders. Looking at birds is not the same as looking at other wildlife. Pocket binoculars are fine for looking across a savannah at an elephant or a cheetah, but they are not suitable for birding. Marine binoculars provide a sharp, bright image, but are too big and heavy to carry around all day.

• Don't buy binoculars until you have tried them. Make sure they feel comfortable in your hands. Look through them and be sure you get a clear, unobstructed view. Different models suit different people, and each instrument varies. If ordering by mail or online, make sure that you can exchange them.

One thing about binoculars – you don't always have to have the best specs for bird watching. Any binoculars are better than none at all. The thing to remember is that you need to have something to magnify the birds you will be looking for. If you are serious about bird watching, take heed of the tips for buying binoculars given above. They will be well worth the money!

Practicing Using Your New Binoculars

Before using your binoculars, it is important to adjust them so they compensate for the differing strengths of your two eyes. Take a lens cap and cover up the right objective lens with it. Then look through the left lens and focus on an object 30 feet away using the main focusing knob located between the two barrels of your binoculars.

Once you have focused on the object, move the lens cap from the right lens to the left lens. Look through the right lens at the same object (but don't touch the main focusing wheel!) If the image you see is not as clear as it looked through the left lens, adjust it using the focusing ring attached to the right eyepiece of your binoculars. Take note of where you have set the focus on the right eyepiece. Now your binoculars are adjusted to your eyes and ready for action.

Next, spend some time developing the hand-eye coordination you'll need to spot birds quickly. Most bird watching is definitely not like watching football. With bird watching there's much more action - everything is happening at 1/100 the scale and moves 100 times as quickly over an unlimited expanse of space. It takes time for beginning birders to get the knack of spotting birds with their binoculars. The secret is to learn to spot a bird with the naked eye and then lift the binoculars up to your eyes without ever taking your eyes off the bird.

Bird Watching Mastery: What You Need To Know About Birds

Find a comfortable spot at a local park and spend time just practicing spotting objects with your binoculars. Initially, set the focus lever on the binoculars so that an object approximately 30 feet away is in clear view. This is a good average distance from which you can learn to focus the binoculars in and out.

Then begin to look for birds with your naked eyes and then find them with your binoculars. Simply follow the bird around for a while, lowering and lifting your binoculars every so often. Don't worry about identifying birds yet. Just watch what they are doing. Soon, you'll be able to spot and focus like a pro.

Field Guides

What is a field guide? A field guide is a little book that's packed with information about birds. It's the next best thing to an expert birder by your side. It describes and shows pictures of the birds, and it tells you which details of each bird to look for.

A field guide can tell you what kinds of birds might be in your particular area and give some excellent tips on what to look for in your bird watching. If you don't have a field guide, you won't have a clue about what kinds of birds you will be seeing, so this is essential to have. A field guide will generally cost you around $20.

A field guide contains pictures of birds and tips for identifying them. The best book for new birders is the Peterson Field Guide to Eastern Birds or the Peterson Field Guide to Western Birds. When you become familiar with the birds in your area, you will probably want the National Geographic Field Guide to the Birds of North America 3rd edition. For young birders, we recommend Peterson First Guide: Birds. It describes 188 common and conspicuous birds and it won't overwhelm you with too many choices. You will also want to look at the new Stokes Field Guides.

Michael Miller

There has been a veritable explosion in the number of field guides published about birds over the last few years. Until the late 1960s, the guide most widely used was Roger Tory Peterson's original The Birds of Eastern North America, the first field guide of its kind produced. This book literally made bird watching a popular activity by making accurate identifications of birds possible.

Today, however, there are specific field guides available for certain regions of the country (Texas even has its own field guide) as well as for specific groups of birds, such as hawks, gulls, shorebirds, ducks, and others. These specialized books may eventually make their way into the library of a birding enthusiast. Still, beginners need only consider the comprehensive guides when choosing their first field guide.

When purchasing your first guide, it is best to start with one that displays paintings of birds rather than photographs. Paintings allow artists to include all distinguishing features (called "field marks") that help to identify a bird in each illustration. Often, photographs do not show all these marks due to lighting or positioning of the bird. Photographic guides can be a valuable companion reference, however, especially when studying the details of a bird's shape.

Once you have selected your field guide, do not - repeat, do not - immediately run off looking for birds, because what you'll actually find instead of birds is trouble and frustration. Many a field guide has spent more time collecting dust than helping to identify birds because the owner didn't learn how to use the guide.

Sit down with your field guide when you first get it and read through the complete introduction. Next, look at some of the pictures and figure out where some of the common birds you recognize are located in the field guide (i.e., front, back, or middle).

Bird Watching Mastery: What You Need To Know About Birds

If you want to become an avid outdoor birder, you'll want a guide that is easy to carry and flip through quickly. If you are more of a backyard birder, watching local species on your feeders and birdbath, portability is not as important.

Field Guide Organization

Numerous beginners tend to spot a bird and immediately open their field guide to the middle pages. They then look to the right ten pages, look left ten pages, and don't find the bird. Then they look right 20 pages, look left 20 pages, and still don't find the bird. After looking a few more pages left and right, they heave the guide into the air out of disgust and give up the whole enterprise.

This happens because the person hasn't learned how bird species are arranged in the field guide. It's no wonder they get frustrated. Field guides, just like dictionaries and phone books, are ordered according to a precise system that determines where different birds are located in the book.

If you were looking up the word "aardvark" in the dictionary, you wouldn't begin somewhere in the middle, would you? Similarly, if you see a sparrow-like bird sitting on the ground, don't start searching through the middle of a field guide because all the sparrows are located in the last quarter of field guides.

Most guides are roughly organized in "phylogenetic order." Phylogenetic order is the way scientists classify all living things (not just birds) based on their evolutionary history - which creatures, according to likenesses in their present-day appearance, most probably evolved from common ancestors.

You can learn more about this ordering system by reading your field guide. The point is that birds having similar physical appearances occur very close together in a field guide. You won't find sparrows on the same page with hawks or a loon facing a warbler. All sparrows, loons, warblers, hawks, and even gulls and blackbirds are located many pages away from one another.

There are five essential levels of classification by which all birds are grouped. When we refer to birds of the same "species," for example a group of 15 blue jays, we are using the most specific level of classification.

Similar species are grouped into a "genus," then different genera (plural of genus) are grouped into a "family," different families are grouped into an "order" of birds, and finally all orders are grouped into just one "class." This is the class "Aves," which in Latin refers to all birds. As you may guess, species in the same genus are more closely related to one another - and look more alike - than species in different genera. Likewise, families grouped in a single order are more similar to one another than families grouped in different orders.

Most field guides covering North America contain about 800-900 species, grouped into over 300 genera, grouped into 74 different families, grouped into just 20 different orders (guides limited to eastern or western North America have about half as many species).

The most convenient and logical classification level for the beginning birder to focus on is the family. There are simply too many genera and species out there for a novice to grasp easily, and identification to a particular order is too broad to be challenging. More importantly, by learning the general shape, size, and appearance of the different families of birds, you will develop the powers of observation that characterize a good birder.

Bird Watching Mastery: What You Need To Know About Birds

In fact, you probably know more about some of the families than you realize. For example, if you can recognize a laughing gull you already know a lot about the general sizes and shapes of all the gulls. Similarly, by knowing what a cardinal looks like, you know a good bit about buntings, grosbeaks, and other members of this family - namely that they have very thick, pointed bills.

Armed with the ability to recognize the shapes of the major bird families and a good local field guide, you can go anywhere in the world and immediately find yourself head and shoulders above non-birders in terms of identification skills - even though you don't have any familiarity or experience with the local birds.

So when you first get your field guide, spend time looking at its organization and the way it group families of birds. Divide your guide into four sections using tags or sticky notes. The first quarter will contain the families of large water birds, the second quarter the large land birds (ending with the woodpeckers), and the last two quarters will contain the small land birds (all in the order "Passeriformes," commonly called the "passerines" or "perching birds").

Continue to look for common species that you already know and use these as a guide for learning the common characteristics of other species in the family. Remember, you should begin birding using your head, not running around chasing after elusive thrushes and confusing fall warblers. Look casually, not frantically, at birds you don't know. Equipped with your spyglasses and trusty field guide, you can now begin to get acquainted with all those flitting bundles of feathers.

Your Notebook

This doesn't have to be anything fancy. We recommend something smaller than the standard 8 x 11 variety. Carry something that is easy to handle and can be kept on your person without being too intrusive.

What do you want to jot down in your notebook? Birds you have seen, where you saw them, what they looked like, what they sounded like, etc. When you record these observations right when you see (and/or hear) them, you will be able to better reflect on your experience later on.

Your Camera

While this is not necessarily considered an essential piece of equipment for bird watching, we think it should be. If you happen across a particularly beautiful species of bird and want to capture it for later study, you could rely on your mind, or you could just snap a picture.

Most of the world is going digital these days. With your digital camera, get one that has the maximum pixels selected for the best pictures. Be sure you have a zoom lens so you can get "up close and personal" with your fine feathered friends. And, by all means, turn off the flash! Nothing can scare away a bird quicker than a flash of light from your camera!

If you have pictures of the birds you see, you can also do more in-depth analysis of the birds once you get home. With pictures, you can delve more deeply into your field guide and document the exact birds you came across in your expedition.

Bird Watching Mastery: What You Need To Know About Birds

And think of the photo album you can create! Beautiful!

Anything Else?

Most experienced bird watchers highly suggest a hat – one that covers your head from the sun and make you less conspicuous. Any old hat will do. Birding is not a fashion contest. But the hat should shade your eyes and not interfere with using your binoculars.

A birding vest is useful, too. You can put your binoculars, your field guide, your pen and notebook, and perhaps some insect repellent in the pockets. Hang the vest near the door, and you'll be ready to grab it and have everything you need for bird watching at a moment's notice.

One last note, when birding, you should wear neutral colored clothing, not white. The last thing you want is to scare away normally skittish creatures with brightly colored clothing that calls attention to the fact that you are there watching them!

Now that you have the right gear, let's look first at some bird watching etiquette.

EMILY POST ON BIRD WATCHING

Armed with knowledge and enthusiasm, you are now ready to head into the field and fill your notebook with dozens of new species. But don't let your eagerness get in the way of basic birding etiquette.

Keep in mind that in order to find most birds you will be encroaching on their territory, so tread lightly and respect boundaries.

Remember that silence is golden. The keen senses of birds alert them to your presence, often long before you have a chance to see them. Whether alone or in a group, walk as quietly as possible and whisper. Take cues from the leader who might signal for quiet as the group approaches a bird. Quiet walks will also help when listening for bird calls.

Take extra care when in a potential or active nesting area. It is hard enough for birds to compete with each other for mates and space; human interference causes additional stress.

Make sure you are not trespassing on private property. Some bird sanctuaries are located on someone's land, whose owners may not enjoy strangers with binoculars trekking around their backyard. Make sure you have the permission to bird beforehand.

Don't be a peeping Tom! Avoid pointing your binoculars at other people or their homes.

While some birders prefer solitude, others bird in groups and enjoy sharing their findings. If you are new to birding, don't be shy; there is sure to be a more knowledgeable birder in the group willing to pass on tips and sightings to you.

Most importantly, enjoy yourself! Don't be too concerned about finding that rare bird, or spotting more species than last month. Birding is meant to be informative, but also fun.

We feel it's important here to quote the American Birding Associations "Principles of Birding Ethics":

Bird Watching Mastery: What You Need To Know About Birds
American Birding Association's

PRINCIPLES OF BIRDING ETHICS

Everyone who enjoys birds and birding must always respect wildlife, its environment, and the rights of others. In any conflict of interest between birds and birders, the welfare of the birds and their environment comes first.

CODE OF BIRDING ETHICS

1. Promote the welfare of birds and their environment.

1(a) Support the protection of important bird habitat.

1(b) To avoid stressing birds or exposing them to danger, exercise restraint and caution during observation, photography, sound recording, or filming.

Limit the use of recordings and other methods of attracting birds, and never use such methods in heavily birded areas, or for attracting any species that is Threatened, Endangered, or of Special Concern, or is rare in your local area;

Keep well back from nests and nesting colonies, roosts, display areas, and important feeding sites. In such sensitive areas, if there is a need for extended observation, photography, filming, or recording, try to use a blind or hide, and take advantage of natural cover.

Use artificial light sparingly for filming or photography, especially for close-ups.

1(c) Before advertising the presence of a rare bird, evaluate the potential for disturbance to the bird, its surroundings, and other people in the area, and proceed only if access can be controlled, disturbance minimized, and permission has been obtained from private land-owners. The sites of rare nesting birds should be divulged only to the proper conservation authorities.

1(d) Stay on roads, trails, and paths where they exist; otherwise keep habitat disturbance to a minimum.

2. Respect the law, and the rights of others.

2(a) Do not enter private property without the owner's explicit permission.

2(b) Follow all laws, rules, and regulations governing use of roads and public areas, both at home and abroad.

2(c) Practice common courtesy in contacts with other people. Your exemplary behavior will generate goodwill with birders and non-birders alike.

3. Ensure that feeders, nest structures, and other artificial bird environments are safe.

3(a) Keep dispensers, water, and food clean, and free of decay or disease. It is important to feed birds continually during harsh weather.

3(b) Maintain and clean nest structures regularly.

3(c) If you are attracting birds to an area ensures the birds are not exposed to predation from cats and other domestic animals, or dangers posed by artificial hazards.

4. Group birding, whether organized or impromptu, requires special care.

Each individual in the group, in addition to the obligations spelled out in Items #1 and #2, has responsibilities as a Group Member.

4(a) Respect the interests, rights, and skills of fellow birders, as well as people participating in other legitimate outdoor activities. Freely share your knowledge and experience, except where code 1(c) applies. Be especially helpful to beginning birders.

4(b) If you witness unethical birding behavior, assesses the situation, and intervenes if you think it prudent. When interceding, inform the person(s) of the inappropriate action, and attempt, within reason, to have it stopped. If the behavior continues, document it, and notify appropriate individuals or organizations.

Group Leader Responsibilities [amateur and professional trips and tours].

4(c) Be an exemplary ethical role model for the group. Teach through word and example.

4(d) Keep groups to a size that limits impact on the environment, and does not interfere with others using the same area.

4(e) Ensure everyone in the group knows of and practices this code.

4(f) Learn and inform the group of any special circumstances applicable to the areas being visited (e.g. no tape recorders allowed).

4(g) Acknowledge that professional tour companies bear a special responsibility to place the welfare of birds and the benefits of public knowledge ahead of the company's commercial interests. Ideally, leaders should keep track of tour sightings, document unusual occurrences, and submit records to appropriate organizations.

PLEASE FOLLOW THIS CODE AND DISTRIBUTE AND TEACH IT TO OTHERS

While it may seem repetitive, it bears repeating just for the simple courtesy of fellow bird watchers as well as those we are watching!

You've got the equipment and know what you should and shouldn't do. Now let's go find some birds!

Chapter 3- Where to Bird Watching?

The beautiful part about birding is that it can truly be done anywhere! You can go to your local park and find some great specimens. If you're traveling, you'll find a new appreciation of the songs of birds and what you can find. You can even watch birds in your own back yard! We'll have more later on in this book about back yard birding.

You need to know what to expect in your area. Checklists of birds in your area will tell you this. Many State and National parks near you have checklists of the birds seen in the park. There are many websites that have checklists for every state and province in the United States and Canada as well as every country in the world! You can find other great sites for birding on the internet.

Learn about the habitat each species of bird prefers. Do they like to spend their time at the top of a tree or on the ground or on a lake? You should learn the songs of the birds in your yard. Later, learn the songs of other birds in your area of the country. To find a bird, you will often hear it first.

You may want to join a group of other birders. Birders are very friendly and helpful. They are always willing to share their knowledge. We were all beginners once. Start by calling the local Audubon Society, the local Nature Center or Parks Commission, or the local Bird Club. If all else fails, go to the park with your binocular. Someone is sure to strike up a conversation and they might lead you to a whole new group of birding buddies.

Try a birding trip or tour. Local bird trips are sometimes advertised in the newspapers. These are often led by park rangers or a local Audubon member. To find out about local trips you should also call your local Rare Bird Alert phone number.

After reciting the list of rare birds seen in the area, they often mention upcoming field trips. The trips may last a morning or most of the day. These trips are usually free of charge. You might also want to join a professional guide on a tour. Tour guides charge for their services but they are worth every penny. Birding tours can take you all over the world.

Birds don't always hang out in classy places; sewage dumps are a favorite. But you needn't start there. Stroll along the beach, in a meadow, by a brook, or on a trail. You'll find birds on the way. One suggestion: avoid dense woods where birds remain hidden. Open areas with trees or hedges are better. Don't forget the zoo. It probably has a pond with ducks and other waterfowl, and they are used to having people around.

Plan a vacation that includes birding. Wherever you go, check out the birding hot spots beforehand and build them into your trip. The bimonthly magazine Bird Watcher's Digest lists vacation spots that cater to birders, and its articles by amateur birders convey the delights of this hobby.

Bird Watching Mastery: What You Need To Know About Birds

Birds aren't always out on a branch in full view; if it was that easy, this wouldn't be a sport! Species can be found at many eye levels, from on the ground to in small shrubs, and from on tree trunks to atop skyscrapers. Once you know what birds live in your area and when, read about what type of habitat they prefer for feeding, breeding and rearing young. Having birdfeeders, birdhouses and birdbaths in your yard certainly makes it easier to see birds.

There are certain times of day when birds are more active than others, depending on the species. The best time to see most birds is usually earlier in the morning; the evening is less productive unless you are looking for nocturnal species, such as owls. Also pay attention to the season. Spring and fall migrations are a great time to spot birds that fly long distances and stopover in your neck of the woods for a rest.

Now that you're outfitted with the equipment and the general knowledge, how can you identify the birds you see?

WHAT KIND OF BIRD IS THAT?

There are hundreds of different birds out there. You probably won't be able to identify every single bird you see. However, armed with some basic information, you can probably narrow down the list and find that you might have a species worth studying.

What should you look for when identifying birds? Becoming an expert on visual identification takes time and patience. Some groups of birds are much easier to definitively identify than others.

The first thing to remember is: don't make bird identification hard on yourself. There are two general rules to keep in mind during your first few months of bird watching: 1) eliminate as many species as possible from consideration before you ever attempt to identify anything, and 2) the bird is most likely a species that commonly occurs in your area, not some strange exotic that blew in from a thousand miles away.

One of the easiest ways to exclude birds is to go through your field guide and put an "X" next to those that do not typically occur in your geographic area. Put these aside for the time being. By doing this, you drastically reduce the number of birds you have to worry about identifying from the 900 birds in your guide to the 300 or so birds that are regularly seen in your location!

By the way, don't worry about marking up your field guide. A field guide personally adjusted to meet your needs is the best friend you can have when alone in the field. Just make sure to use a pencil or permanent ink so that the words won't smear if you leave the book in the rain or drop it in the mud occasionally.

Another way to eliminate choices is to consider the time of year the bird might occur in your area. The range maps included with field guides display this type of information. Some beginners might even find it beneficial to place colored dots next to birds in their field guides.

For example, put a red dot next to birds that are year-round residents, put a blue dot next to birds that are only winter visitors, put a green dot next to birds that are summer visitors, and put a black dot next to birds that only pass through during migration.

CLUES TO IDENTIFICATION

The way that some birds skulk about, you'd think that they were afraid of showing off their pretty colors and didn't want anyone to identify them. And this is the case, no doubt, as they must somehow evade predators from both above and below. Often,

Bird Watching Mastery: What You Need To Know About Birds
their quick movements allow us only a glimpse. Still, you will be able to identify even the most secretive bird using the key clues to identification described here.

There are five basic clues you can look and listen for that will allow you to solve the bird identification puzzle: 1) the bird's silhouette, 2) its plumage and coloration, 3) its behavior, 4) its habitat preferences, and 5) its voice. This may seem like a formidable amount of information to gather, but in truth you often need only one or two of these clues to identify a bird.

Sometimes, the key to identification is as easy as knowing which clue to look for first when you see an unusual bird. As your birding abilities increase, you will be able to pinpoint the important clues with greater ease and certainty.

Silhouette - Shape and Size

As you become familiar with your field guide, you will be able to quickly categorize most birds into families using silhouette alone (remember, each family has a diagnostic shape and size).

This will immediately put you at an advantage compared to the average observer because by placing the bird you see into a particular family, you have already narrowed down the possible birds you could be seeing from the 900 in your field guide to only about 15 or so birds - the 15 birds within the family you have identified. As mentioned earlier, you can then further eliminate any species in the family that do not occur in your region during that season.

You can do this even in the worst of lighting conditions when birds are backlit, in low light, or in shadow. It doesn't matter. The overall shape is unchanged. Many birds are even identifiable to species by outline alone.

Of course, it will not be easy to accomplish this feat at first. You must learn to note carefully all the details of a bird's shape. Is the bird large or small, short-legged or long-legged, crested or not crested, plump or slim and sleek, short-tailed or long-tailed? Note every detail in your field notebook.

The shape of a bird's bill is also an extremely helpful clue that is obvious from a silhouette. Cardinals, finches, and sparrows have short conical bills. Woodpeckers have chisel-shaped bills for working dead wood. Hawks, eagles, and falcons, on the other hand, have sharp, hooked bills that make quick work of meat. Shorebirds have slender bills of all lengths for probing at different depths into the sand.

The beak is a telltale sign. It indicates whether the bird cracks seeds (short, thick beak), drills for grubs (long, pointed beak), picks stuff off leaves (short, thin beak), and so forth. Your bird guide can help you identify beak shapes.

Size is also an important field mark and field guides do list the size of birds next to pictures. However, if you don't have some type of scale in mind, these numbers are of little use. The "ruler" many birders use in the field is a mental association of three familiar birds with three general size classes.

For example, a house sparrow is 5-6 inches in size, a northern mockingbird is 9-11 inches in size, and an American crow is 17-21 inches in size. Now, using phrases like "larger than a crow" or "smaller than a sparrow," you have an immediate impression of the approximate size of any bird. You also have an immediate frame of

Bird Watching Mastery: What You Need To Know About Birds
reference for your field guide if you associate each of these three species with 5, 10, and 20-inch size classes.

Plumage

Plumage characteristics are what really draw a lot of people into bird watching - they like seeing those beautiful colors. The distinguishing plumage clues that identify different species are known as "field marks." These include such things as breast spots, wing bars (thin lines along the wings), eye rings (circles around the eyes), eyebrows (lines over the eyes), eye lines (lines through the eyes) and many others.

Some field marks are best seen when a bird is in flight. A flying northern harrier can be identified from nearly a mile away with good binoculars because the bird has a bright white patch on its rump.

Some families of birds can be broken into even smaller groups based on one or two simple field marks. For example, warblers are fairly evenly divided between those that have wing bars and those that do not. So if you see a warbler-like bird, look quickly to see if it has wing bars. Sparrows, on the other hand, can be separated into two smaller groups based on whether or not the breast is streaked. Look for other broad distinctions for other families.

Behavior

A bird's behavior - how it flies, forages, or generally comports itself - is one of the best clues to its identity.

Hawks have a "serious" demeanor, crows and jays are "gregarious," and cuckoos are... well, not really. Woodpeckers climb up the sides of tree trunks searching for grubs like a lineman scaling a telephone pole.

Flycatchers, on the other hand, wouldn't climb a tree trunk if their lives depended on it. They spend most of their time sitting upright on an exposed perch. When they see a bug cruising into range they quickly dart from their perch, snag the meal, and then return to the same perch or another one nearby.

Finches spend a lot of their time on the ground in search of fallen seeds, as do mockingbirds, catbirds, and brown thrashers. Some wading birds, such as snowy egrets and reddish egrets, are very active foragers and chase their prey around in shallow waters. Other wading birds, such as great blue herons, are less impetuous and hunt slowly with great patience and stealth.

Even the way a bird props its tail gives some clues as to which species or family it might be. Wrens characteristically hold their tails in a cocked position and often bounce from side to side.

Spotted sandpipers and Louisiana water thrushes bounce their tails and rumps rapidly up and down as if doing a stylish dance step. Some thrushes and flycatchers, on the other hand, move their tails frequently but slowly, with a wave-like motion.

You can even identify some birds just by the way that they fly. Most finches and woodpeckers move through the air with an undulating flight pattern, flapping their wings for short bursts and then tucking them under for a short rest.

One group of raptors, the buteos or soaring hawks, circle the sky suspended on outstretched wings. Most falcons, another group of raptors, fly with strong wing beats and rarely hover. Yet another group, the accipiters or bird hawks, usually fly in a straight line with alternating periods of flapping and floating.

Habitat

Even if a range map shows that a bird occurs in your neck of the woods, this doesn't mean the bird will be common wherever you go. Birds segregate themselves according to habitat type and are sometimes quite picky in selecting an area as home.

Wading birds and ducks, for example, prefer watery habitats rather than dry upland areas. Pine warblers and brown-headed nuthatches associate primarily with pinewoods and are less common in areas containing large numbers of oaks, hickories, and other deciduous trees.

Beginning bird watchers must usually spend many hours in the field before they are able to associate different species with different habitat types. You should develop a key to habitats you frequent and keep notes of where you see different species.

Make the habitat key simple at first, using terms like salt and freshwater marsh, pinelands, deciduous forest, beach, urban area, farm and pastureland, etc. Then elaborate on this key as you learn to distinguish among different habitat types.

You can put abbreviations such as "SM" (for salt water marsh), "PW" (for pinewoods), and "FP" (for farm and pasture) next to the pictures of birds in your field guide after you have some feel for where the birds occur. Most field guides actually provide this information in the written description but this abbreviated system may help you remember the habitats where each bird occurs.

Voice

Birds have unique songs and calls and voice is often all that's needed to identify many of the birds you encounter. If each species didn't have a distinctive call or song, there would be a lot of confusion out there when birds tried to communicate. Just as you can tell that the person on the other end of the phone is Uncle Bob and not Aunt Edith, so too can you learn to distinguish the different voices of birds.

Listening to recordings helps considerably when you are trying to learn bird vocalizations. Many are currently available on tape and CD. You can also find them online.

However, no matter how many recordings you listen to, there is no substitute for going out into the field. There's something about the association of voice and bird that helps to fix both in memory. Plus, bird vocalizations are complex and no set of recordings can hope to encompass all the variety and geographic variations that can be experienced firsthand out in nature.

Keep all of these aspects in your notebook, recording the bird's features as you watch it. Watch it as long as you can. Write down your description while it's fresh. Then, look in your field guide for further identification.

In general, you should try to keep the following points in mind when trying to identify the birds you see.

Begin by focusing on those groups that are both common and distinctive, and then, when you see an unknown species take a visual inventory of its unique characteristics. How large is it? What is the shape of the body? Does it walk, hop, waddle or wade? Notice the shape of its beak. Is it long, narrow, stalky, flat or

Bird Watching Mastery: What You Need To Know About Birds

hooked? Is there a crest on the head? Does the tail extend beyond the body? Is the tip round, square, forked or fan shaped? Take a careful inventory of the colors of the bird. In particular look at the head, wings, and tail. In flight, the color of the rear edge of the wing, or speculum, is one of the key identifiers for waterfowl.

When the bird moves, take note of its behavior. This is often as distinctive as its physical appearance. How does it hold its tail? Is it found on the ground, perched in trees, or soaring high above? When perched, does it hold its body upright or horizontal? Does it use its tail as a brace as in woodpeckers? If it climbs along the trunk, does it tend to climb up the tree or down?

If it lives in and around the water notice how it swims. Does it merely tip its bill into the water leaving its tail above the surface, or does it dive completely underwater? When it takes off, does it jump straight into the air or does it require a long runway to become airborne? If it wades, take note of how long its legs are. Does it slowly stalk like a heron or rapidly run along the shoreline probing with its beak? Does it bob up and down like a dipper or teeter like a spotted sandpiper?

When airborne, does it have a constant rhythm or does it undulate like a woodpecker? Does it generally fly in a straight line or perform aerial acrobatics like a swallow? How fast does it beat its wings? Is it alone or in a flock?

Also taking note of the habitat and season may help identify a bird, or at least help distinguish between two similar species. Birds are generally migratory, appearing in large flocks on open water in the fall and spring. Knowing their habitat and annual cycles can often form the last key element in identification.

If it was feeding, determine if its food was nectar, fruit, insects, seeds, or other creatures.

A few other things to consider when identifying birds:

- It's what you notice first, but color is unreliable. A bird's color changes dramatically in different light conditions. So don't rely on color alone when you try to identify the bird in a guide.

- Check the range. You may think you've identified the bird, but make sure it should be there. Beginning birders make amazing finds-sometimes the only example of a species to be seen in that region. Your birding guide should give ranges for different species. Make sure your bird belongs.

- Don't try to locate a bird only by sound. They're ventriloquists. And don't scan the trees with your binoculars. Instead, watch for movement, and then aim your binoculars. Fast. Even if you've got one of those pesky, flitting warbler species, keep trying. You'll get it.

- If you just can't spot it, forget it. Remember this rule: Any bird you didn't see was a robin.

Don't forget to pay special attention to the song of the bird. This could be a main component in identifying the bird you have seen.

Chapter 4 - Bird Watching Mastery with Your Ears

A bird does not sing because it has an answer. It sings because it has a song.

> ~Chinese Proverb

A bird's song can be beautiful music or a screeching annoyance. Its tune can help you identify what kind of bird it is and where to look for it in your field guide. All you need is to tune in to their songs. Each species makes sounds that are unique, and you can identify the birds by those sounds just as easily as you can by their shape or color.

Indeed, there are advantages to birding by ear. You can do it in the dark (a useful skill for identifying owls when you're camping). The barred owl, for example, sounds completely different from any other sound you hear at night.

A bird hidden in dense summer foliage will often sing out its identity for all who have ears to hear. And although you can see with your eyes only in the direction you happen to be facing, you can hear in all directions at once, so you can identify a bird by its song even when it's behind your back.

We humans live in a different sensory world from most creatures of earth. Your dog, for example experiences the world mainly through his nose, while our sense of smell is puny by comparison. It's difficult even to imagine the sensory impressions taken in by bats or beetles, frogs or fish.

On the other hand, birds' strongest senses are sight and hearing, and they have evolved ways to communicate and to recognize their own species by using signals based on those two senses. Because we are also creatures of sight and sound, we can tap right into all the fascinating distinctions of color and shape that birds embody, and just as naturally we can appreciate the sounds that are so important in their lives.

As you begin to recognize bird songs, you will bring yourself into a whole new dimension of bird watching. You will probably find yourself mesmerized by the sing-song voice of the bird outside your window and recognize birds you didn't know you had around you!

Get a field guide to bird songs. Just as you need a book with pictures to learn what birds look like, you need recordings to learn what they sing like. Fortunately, there are several excellent tapes and CDs of bird songs available now. You can also find some excellent resources online for bird songs. Familiarize yourself with these songs and open yourself to a whole new world of bird watching!

When you hear a bird's song, describe it to yourself in words. You might notice that the white-breasted nuthatch has a nasal sound to his "Yenk, yenk, yenk" song, and that each note of the northern cardinal's song is a slippery, downward slurp, or that the blue jay's call is sometimes loud and harsh, as if the bird were screaming "Thief!" Making mental note of such characteristics helps you recognize the bird when you hear it again.

Associate a phrase of English with the song, such as "Peter, Peter, Peter" for the tufted titmouse. The words will remind you of the rhythm, speed, or pitch of the song.

Bird Watching Mastery: What You Need To Know About Birds

It's best when you can fit your own words to a bird's song, but feel free to use memorable phrases others come up with. The ovenbird is traditionally reputed to sing out "teacher, Teacher, TEACHER," and it's hard to improve on "Quick, three beers!" for the olive-sided flycatcher's call.

Once you ascribe words to a bird's song, the melody stays with you forever. Chicago may no longer mean just a city in Illinois; it might be the song of that unique bird you found last week.

After you've become familiar with a few songs, make a point of listening early in the morning. During the hour before sunrise, many birds sing. The chorus is lovely to listen to as a whole, but it is also a pleasure to single out and recognize the individual voices in the choir. Some birds sing throughout the day, but you'll hear 100 times as much bird song first thing in the morning as at noon.

At any season, you can see more birds with your ears than you can with your eyes. So why not give it a go tomorrow morning? Sleep with a window open, so that you'll hear the birds singing when you first wake up. If you don't know what they are, try to separate out one song from the rest. Even though the singer may remain a mystery to you for a while, it will serve as your inspiration to learn to see with your ears.

You don't necessarily have to travel to find birds. You can attract many species of birds to your home – right in your own backyard. What could be better than sitting on your porch and pursuing bird watching in the comfort of your own home?

BACKYARD BIRDING

Among the fondest and most memorable moments of childhood are the discoveries of songbirds nesting in the backyard. The distinctive, mud-lined nests of robins and their beautiful blue eggs captivate people of all ages. Likewise, the nesting activities of house wrens, cardinals, chickadees, and other common birds can stimulate a lifelong interest in nature.

As you learn to enjoy the beauty of birdlife around your home, you may wish to improve the "habitat" in your yard so that more birds will visit your property. You can attract birds by placing bird feeders, nest boxes, and bird baths in your yard, and by planting a variety of trees, shrubs, and flowers. These can provide good nesting sites, winter shelter, places to hide from predators and natural food supplies that are available year-round.

There are a few different ways to attract varieties of birds to your yard. These can include planting certain flowers, installing a bird feeder, or putting out a bird bath.

You can do backyard birding and attract birds to your yard by providing appropriate food, water, and habitats for wild birds, and limiting use of pesticides. Bushes and dense hedges protect birds from predators, provide perches, and are home to insects, which are great bird food. Colorful flowers also attract hummingbirds

It doesn't matter where you live - in an apartment, townhouse or single family dwelling, in the city, suburbs or country. Just stand still and you'll hear them: wild birds. It is hard to imagine life without them

BIRD FEEDERS

There are several factors to consider after you've decided to feed birds in your backyard.

Bird Watching Mastery: What You Need To Know About Birds

Where do you want to watch your birds? From a kitchen window ... a sliding glass door opening onto a deck ... a second-story window?

Pick a location that is easy to get to. When the weather is bad and birds are most vulnerable, you may be reluctant to fill a feeder that is not in a convenient spot near a door or an accessible window. Also, pick a site where discarded seed shells and bird droppings won't be a cleanup problem.

Put your feeder where the squirrels can't reach. Squirrels become a problem when they take over a bird feeder, scaring the birds away and tossing seed all over. Squirrels have been known to chew right through plastic and wooden feeders.

If you've seen squirrels in your neighborhood, it is safe to assume they will visit your feeder. Think long and hard before you hang anything from a tree limb. Squirrels are incredibly agile, and any feeder hanging from a tree is likely to become a squirrel feeder.

In the long run, a squirrel-proof feeder or any feeder on a pole with a baffle is the least aggravating solution. The most effective squirrel-proof feeder is the pole-mounted metal "house" type.

what kind of bird food should you use? The hands-down favorite bird seed is sunflower. It attracts cardinals, woodpeckers, blue jays, goldfinches, purple finches, chickadees, titmice, and nuthatches. Get the black sunflower seeds, sometimes called oil seeds. Birds prefer them to the grey-and-white-striped sunflower seeds sold off the candy rack for people, because they're higher in oil content. They are softer shelled, hence easier to crack open. They're also cheaper than the grey-and-white ones.

Another essential bird seed is niger. Goldfinches adore niger. Niger is a black seed, so tiny and light you can blow away a handful with a gentle breath. Niger is also expensive, over a dollar a pound, so you won't want to waste it. Buy a hanging tube with tiny holes, designed especially for niger, and hang it where you can see it from your best viewing window. Up close to the house, even under the eaves, is fine. Goldfinches will become very tame and won't mind you stand two feet away from them, on the other side of the window, while they eat.

Another favorite seeds for birds is safflower, a white seed, slightly smaller than a black sunflower seed. Squirrels don't like it. Neither do grackles, blue jays, or starlings. Safflower seeds are extremely bitter. Cardinals, titmice, chickadees, and downy woodpeckers munch it like candy, though, so keep a good supply available on the platform feeder. The squirrels won't bother to climb up there as well.

White millet is another seed that attracts birds. It is even cheaper than sunflower seed. Scatter it on the ground for sparrows, juncos, and mourning doves.

You can buy these seeds at feed stores, nurseries, supermarkets, and some hardware stores. It's a good idea to buy everything except the costly niger in 50-pound bags and store them in the garage in mouse-proof metal trash cans.

Don't bother with bags of mixed birdseed. These mixes usually contain a lot of filler, such as red millet. Most birds won't eat it. They rummage through the seeds in the feeder and kick the red millet onto the ground, where at best it lies until it rots and turns into pretty decent fertilizer for the grass. Mixed birdseed is not a bargain. Buy the seeds you know your birds want.

When starting up a feeding program, be patient. It may take as long as several weeks before the birds discover your feeders. While you wait, be sure to keep the feeders filled. Eventually, the birds will come.

Sometimes conscientious people are concerned about whether feeding the birds will harm the birds. Will the birds become dependent on the handouts? And it's often advised that one should only start feeding birds if certain that the feeding can continue uninterrupted.

However, the evidence indicates that feeding is not likely to be bad for birds. They don't settle in and dine at just one place. Goldfinches, for example, follow a circuit each day, visiting a number of feeders and wild food patches, as we know from studies of banded birds that can be identified individually.

With many households feeding birds, it's unlikely that a bird will starve because one feeder goes empty. All the same, birds that come into your yard at dusk are hungry, and it is bad manners to disappoint guests! Make sure they have enough to dine on at your pleasure!

Birds like to feed on hanging suet molds. You can buy these in many different place, but this can be especially fun if you can make them yourself. They're so easy, even the children can help! Make a simple bird feeder by attaching a short length of string to a pine cone, covering the pine cone with a suet, lard, or vegetable shortening mixture (see below), and rolling it in seeds, and then suspending it from a tree branch.

Fatty mixture: Mix 1/2 cup suet, lard, or vegetable shortening with 2 1/2 cups cornmeal or uncooked oats until well blended. Optional: add dried fruit (chopped up), chopped nuts, and/or 1/4 cup finely chopped leftover meat (only in cold weather).

Hummingbirds drink nectar which is also easy to make yourself. Take ¼ cup sugar and dissolve in boiling water. Place into your hummingbird feeder and watch them come! Be sure to change the nectar often as – especially in warm weather – the mixture can become rancid and dangerous for the birds. Also, hummingbirds tend to enjoy red nectar the best, so add a few drops of food coloring to the mixture!

Don't forget water! The best way to provide water to your feathered friends is with a bird bath.

BACKYARD BIRD BATHS

Kindness is a birdbath. Your little circle of clean, cool water under a leafy branch is a kindness to the birds, because fresh clean water can sometimes be the hardest necessity for birds to come by. And it's a kindness to yourself and your family, too, because watching the birds at the birdbath will bring you great happiness.

In fact, a birdbath is one of the easiest ways to bring birds up close, where you can get a really good look at them. You can attract even more species of birds with water than with a feeder.

Bird feeders usually cater to seed-eaters, such as cardinals, blue jays, and sparrows. Birds that eat insects or fruit, such as wrens, catbirds, and waxwings, usually don't find anything at the feeder to interest them. But the birdbath entices all kinds of birds, from robins to screech owls. It will expand your awareness of the variety of life.

Commercial bird baths are available at many discount stores and gardening or home improvement store, but you can make a birdbath out of almost anything. Just make sure it provides what the birds need most – cool, clean water!

Bird Watching Mastery: What You Need To Know About Birds

What kind of birdbath is best? It needs to be shallow - no deeper than three inches at the center. It should be even shallower at the edge, so that a bird can ease its way in. Many commercial birdbaths are too deep. If you already own a deep birdbath, you can put rocks in it to raise the bottom, though this will make it a little harder to keep clean.

Consider adding a fountain or something to provide a bit of a drip. The plinking sound of falling water is pure invitation to birds. It dramatically increases the number of species that visit a birdbath. For example, hummingbirds would never wade into the bath like other birds, because they bathe only in flight. But many have watched hummers zipping back and forth through the drips of a bird bath, timing their flights so that they catch a water drop on their backs on each pass.

There are many ways to arrange for a drip. You can run a hose so that it trickles into the water; or install a small spray fountain designed for birdbaths; or suspend above the bath a bucket that has a 1/2-inch hole in the bottom with a bit of cloth stuffed through the hole as a wick.

Also make sure your bird bath is rough bottomed. Birds don't want to lose their footing, and they will hesitate to use a bath with a glazed, slippery bottom. Cement is good. If you already possess a slick birdbath, you can apply the non-skid stickers that are sold for people-baths.

Place your bird bath within view from a window. Don't forget to put yourself in this picture. Place the birdbath where you can see it from indoors, from your desk, dining room, or kitchen sink. Put the basin on a pedestal. It's easy to see from the house, easy to clean, and safer from predators. Alternatively, you can buy a birdbath designed to hang from a tree.

Make your birdbath easy to clean and refill by placing it close enough to reach with a hose. However, locate your birdbath away from your feeding station, because seeds and droppings would spoil the water quickly. Change the water every few days, or even every day in hot weather. Dump it out or squirt it out with the hose. It's a good idea to keep a scrub brush outside with gardening tools, so that you can brush out any algae that might begin to form.

Place the bird bath where predators cannot get to your visitors. Cats, for example, like to lie in wait beneath shrubbery or behind a concealing object and then pounce on the birds when they're wet and can't fly well. So put your birdbath at least five to ten feet from such hiding places. Give the birds a chance to see the cat coming. Also provide the birds with an escape route. The ideal location is under some branches that hang down within two or three feet of the bath. A wet bird can flutter a few feet up to the safety of the leaves.

If you follow these instructions, soon a robin will land on the rim of your birdbath. He'll dip his bill into the water and then raise his head to let the water run down inside his throat. Then he'll hop in and splash exuberantly. He'll dunk his head and let the water rush over his back. He'll sit and soak.

When he's finished bathing, he'll fly onto the nearest branch, where he'll shake off and begin to preen his feathers, drawing them one by one through his bill.

A bird in the bath is the soul of enjoyment. The sight of it, even a chance glimpse through the window, will provide you too with a splash of happiness.

Chapter 5- Bird Watching Mastery and Bird Houses

You might decide you don't want your birds to just drop by to eat and take a bath. Perhaps you'd like it if they'd stick around while. Try putting up a bird house or two.

In the bird house business, there's no such thing as "one size fits all." Decide which bird you want to attract, and then get a house for that particular bird. Look through any book or catalog and you'll see bird houses of all sizes and shapes, with perches and without, made of materials you might not have thought of: recycled paper, gourds, plastic, rubber, pottery, metal and concrete. The proper combination of quality materials and design makes a good birdhouse

Wood is just about the best building material for any birdhouse. It's durable, has good insulating qualities and breathes. Three-quarter-inch thick bald cypress and red cedar are recommended. Pine and exterior grade plywood will do, but they are not as durable. It makes no difference whether the wood is slab, rough-cut or finished, as long as the inside has not been treated with stains or preservatives. Fumes from the chemicals could harm the birds.

You can decorate the outside of your birdhouse however you want. Do you want your martins to hang out in a Victorian home or have your cardinal's roost in a clubhouse? Anything goes as far as the outside of the house is concerned. Don't put an aluminum roof on your bird house, however. The glare from the sun will cause birds to shy away. Be sure to provide ventilation, drainage, and easy access for maintenance and monitoring.

How elaborate you make your bird house depends on your own tastes. In addition to where you place the box, the most important considerations are: box height, depth, floor dimensions, diameter of entrance hole and height of the hole above the box floor.

You should provide air vents in bird boxes. There are two ways to provide ventilation: leave gaps between the roof and sides of the box, or drill 1/4 inch holes just below the roof.

Water becomes a problem when it sits in the bottom of a bird house. A roof with sufficient slope and overhang offers some protection. Drilling the entrance hole on an upward slant may also help keep the water out. Regardless of design, driving rain will get in through the entrance hole. You can assure proper drainage by cutting away the corners of the box floor and drilling 1/4 inch holes. Nest boxes will last longer if the floors are recessed about 1/4 inch.

Look for the entrance hole on the front panel near the top. A rough surface both inside and out makes it easier for the adults to get into the box and, when it's time, for the nestlings to climb out.

Bird Watching Mastery: What You Need To Know About Birds

If your box is made of finished wood, add a couple of grooves outside below the hole. Open the front panel and add grooves, cleats or wire mesh to the inside. Never put up a bird house with a perch below the entrance hole.

Perches offer starlings, house sparrows and other predators a convenient place to wait for lunch. Don't be tempted by duplexes or houses that have more than one entrance hole. Except for purple martins, cavity-nesting birds prefer not to share a house. While these condos look great in your yard, starlings and house sparrows are inclined to use them.

Where you put your bird house is as important as its design and construction. Cavity-nesting birds are very particular about where they live. If you don't have the right habitat, the birds are not likely to find the house. You can modify your land to attract the birds you want to see by putting out a bird bath, planting fruit-bearing shrubs, including more trees or installing a pond with a waterfall.

Don't put bird houses near bird feeders. Houses mounted on metal poles are less vulnerable to predators than houses nailed to tree trunks or hung from tree limbs.

Use no more than four small nest boxes or one large box per acre for any one species. Don't put more than one box in a tree unless the tree is extremely large or the boxes are for different species. If you have very hot summers, face the entrance holes of your boxes north or east to avoid overheating the box.

You can also attract some unique species of birds by simply landscaping your yard to attract birds.

LANDSCAPING FOR BIRDS

As people learn to enjoy the beauty of birds around their home, they may wish to improve the "habitat" in their yard so that more birds will visit their property. We've already addressed improving their habitat with bird houses, feeders, and baths. Now let's look at planting a variety of trees, shrubs, and flowers to attract birds. These can provide good nesting sites, winter shelter, places to hide from predators and natural food supplies that are available year-round.

Beautiful landscaping isn't only for attracting birds. It can increase your property value, provide natural beauty, and become a playground for young ones as various wildlife is attracted to your yard.

Landscaping for birds involves nine basic principles:

Food

Every bird species has its own unique food requirements that may change as the seasons change. Learn the food habits of the birds you wish to attract. Then plant the appropriate trees, shrubs, and flowers to provide the fruits, berries, seeds, acorns, and nectar.

Water

You may be able to double the number of bird species in your yard by providing a source of water. A frog pond, water garden, or bird bath will get lots of bird use, especially if the water is dripping, splashing or moving.

Bird Watching Mastery: What You Need To Know About Birds

Shelter

Birds need places where they can hide from predators and escape from severe weather. Trees (including dead ones), shrubs, tall grass and bird houses provide excellent shelter.

Diversity

The best landscaping plan is one that includes a variety of native plants. This helps attract the most bird species.

Four Seasons

Give the birds food and shelter throughout the year by planting a variety of trees, shrubs and flowers that provide year-round benefits.

Arrangement

Properly arrange the different habitat components in your yard. Consider the effects of prevailing winds (and snow drifting) so your yard will be protected from harsh winter weather.

Protection

Birds should be protected from unnecessary mortality. When choosing the placement of bird feeders and nest boxes, consider their accessibility to predators. Picture windows can also be dangerous for birds. They tend to fly directly at windows when they see the reflection of trees and shrubs.

A network of parallel, vertical strings spaced 4 inches apart can be placed on the outside of windows to prevent this problem. Be cautious about the kinds of herbicides and pesticides used in your yard. Apply them only when necessary and strictly according to label instructions. In fact, try gardening and lawn care without using pesticides. Details can be found in gardening books at the library.

Hardiness Zones

When considering plants not native to your area, consult a plant hardiness zone map, found in most garden catalogues. Make sure the plants you want are rated for the winter hardiness zone classification of your area.

Soils and Topography

Consult your local garden center, university or county extension office to have your soil tested. Plant species are often adapted to certain types of soils. If you know what type of soil you have, you can identify the types of plants that will grow best in your yard.

Seven types of plants are important as bird habitat:

Conifers

Conifers are evergreen trees and shrubs that include pines, spruces, firs, arborvitae, junipers, cedars, and yews. These plants are important as escape cover, winter shelter and summer nesting sites. Some also provide sap, fruits and seeds.

Grasses and Legumes

Grasses and legumes can provide cover for ground nesting birds-but only if the area is not mowed during the nesting season. Some grasses and legumes provide seeds as well. Native prairie grasses are becoming increasingly popular for landscaping purposes.

Bird Watching Mastery: What You Need To Know About Birds

Nectar-producing Plants

Nectar-producing plants are very popular for attracting hummingbirds and orioles. Flowers with tubular red corollas are especially attractive to hummingbirds. Other trees, shrubs, vines and flowers also can provide nectar for hummingbirds.

Summer-fruiting Plants

This category includes plants that produce fruits or berries from May through August. In the summer these plants can attract brown thrashers, catbirds, robins, thrushes, waxwings, woodpeckers, orioles, cardinals, towhees and grosbeaks. Examples of summer-fruiting plants are various species of cherry, chokecherry, honeysuckle, raspberry, serviceberry, blackberry, blueberry, grape, mulberry, plum and elderberry

Fall-fruiting Plants

This landscape component includes shrubs and vines whose fruits ripen in the fall. These foods are important both for migratory birds which build up fat reserves before migration and as a food source for non-migratory species that need to enter the winter season in good physical condition. Fall-fruiting plants include dogwoods, mountain ash, winter-berries, cotton Easters and buffalo-berries.

Winter-fruiting Plants

Winter-fruiting plants are those whose fruits remain attached to the plants long after they first become ripe in the fall. Many are not palatable until they have frozen and thawed many times. Examples are glossy black chokecherry, Siberian and "red splendor" crabapple, snowberry, bittersweet, sumacs, American high bush cranberry, eastern and European Wahoo, Virginia creeper, and Chinaberry

Nut and Acorn Plants

These include oaks, hickories, buckeyes, chestnuts, butternuts, walnuts and hazels. A variety of birds, such as jays, woodpeckers and titmice, eat the meats of broken nuts and acorns. These plants also contribute to good nesting habitat.

How do you get started now that you're armed with this vast knowledge of plants that attract birds? Your goal will be to plant an assortment of trees, shrubs and flowers that will attract birds. If you plan carefully it can be inexpensive and fun for the whole family.

First, set your priorities. Decide what types of birds you wish to attract, and then build your plan around the needs of those species. Talk to friends and neighbors to find out what kinds of birds frequent your area. Attend a local bird club meeting and talk to local birdwatchers about how they have attracted birds to their yards.

Whenever possible, use plants native to your area. Check with the botany department of a nearby college or university or with your state's natural heritage program for lists of trees, shrubs, and wildflowers native to your area. Use this list as a starting point for your landscape plan.

These plants are naturally adapted to the climate of your area and are a good long-term investment. Many native plants are both beautiful for landscaping purposes and excellent for birds. If you include normative plant species in your plan, be sure they are not

Bird Watching Mastery: What You Need To Know About Birds
considered "invasive pests" by plant experts. Check out the bird books in your local library.

Sketch a drawing of your property as a map to start with. Sketch on your map the plants you wish to add. Draw trees to a scale that represents three-fourths of their mature width, and shrubs at their full mature width. This will help you calculate how many trees and shrubs you need.

There is a tendency to include so many trees that eventually your yard will be mostly shaded. Be sure to leave open sunny sites where flowers and shrubs can thrive. Decide how much money you can spend and the time span of your project. Don't try to do too much at once. You might try a five-year development plan.

Review the seven plant components described previously. Which components are already present? Which ones are missing? Remember that you are trying to provide food and cover through all four seasons. Develop a list of plants that you think will provide the missing habitat components.

Finally, go to it! Begin your plantings and include your entire family so they can all feel they are helping wildlife. Document your plantings on paper and by photographs. Try taking pictures of your yard from the same spots every year to document the growth of your plants.

Keep your landscaping looking great! Keep your new trees, shrubs and flowers adequately watered, and keep your planting areas weed-free by use of landscaping film and wood chips or shredded bark mulch. This avoids the use of herbicides for weed control. If problems develop with your plants, consult a local nursery, garden center or county extension agent.

Chapter 6- Know the Prominent Contributors and Organization to Bird Watching

Though the sport of birding is more a collaborative effort of many, there are a few people that stand out. These individuals have made various notable contributions to both the sport of birding as well as birding publications. These four have helped to increase the understanding and further the interest to many enthusiasts. It has to be noted though that many have contributed to the world of birding, and that these mentioned individuals are just a few in a long list.

Roger Tory Peterson

Roger Tory Peterson was truly an inspiration to bird enthusiasts everywhere. Peterson was born in Jamestown, New York in 1908. He went onto further his education at the Art Students League and National Academy of Design. He then went on to teach school in Massachusetts. In 1904 when Peterson was only 26 years old, he wrote the first modern field guide titled "Field Guide to the Bird"

Bird Watching Mastery: What You Need To Know About Birds
which resulted in inspiring many enthusiasts. It actually sold out its first printing in the first week alone.

Peterson went on to either write or edit close to 50 books on the topic of nature in one form or another. Peterson revolutionized the modern bird guides with a sense of clarity and understanding that failed to exist before him. Peterson was awarded every kind of American award existing for his studies and literature in natural science, ornithology, and conservation. Not to mention all the other awards and diplomas presented to him from both within the United States and beyond. Many have described him as one of monumental significance in the promotion of all living creatures and nature. Peterson died in 1996 while in his home in Connecticut.

Kenn Kaufman

Kenn Kaufman was born in 1954 in South Bend, Indiana. Kaufman had a love of birds from the early age of six. When he was sixteen he so loved the field of birding and was inspired by greats in the field such as Roger Tory Peterson that he withdrew from high school and began to travel North America in search of birds. In 1973 he set the precedent recording as many as 671 bird species in North America in as little as one year. He was the first to complete such a feat. He journey across North America encompassed around eighty thousand miles. A detail of his journey is recorded in "Kingbird Highway."

Kaufman's main focus was on that of creating and expanding birding field guides. A few pieces of his work include "Kaufman Focus Guides: Birds of North America"," Lives of American Birds", and "The Peterson Guide to Advanced Birding". In 1992 he was recognized by the

American Birding Association when he was awarded the Ludlow Griscom Award for Outstanding Contributions to American Ornithology.

Phoebe Snetsinger

Phoebe Snetsinger was born in 1931 in Lake Zurich, Illinois. Snetsinger was an inspiration to many in the birding community. She is the first person to have seen over 8,000 species before she died. Her fascination of birding began in 1965 after observing a Blackburnian Warbler. Although interested, she did not begin to ardently pursue her birding fascination until 1981 when she was diagnosed with terminal melanoma. Presented with the dire news, she chose continue living her life while fulfilling her passion for birding.

Snetsinger threw herself into her quest to observe as many birds as possible before her time was up. She traveled all over the world while encountering all types of danger throughout her quest. It was during a birding trip in 1999 that Snetsinger was killed in a tragic car accident. During her travels she made it a habit to take notes of all her experiences as well as findings. After her death the book "Birding on Borrowed Time" was published in 2003 with accounts of Snetsinger's travels as well as her fight with an incurable illness.

Theodore A. Parker III

Theodore A Parker III was born in 1953 and raised in Lancaster, Pennsylvania. Parker became interested in bird watching while quite young, and at age 18 broke the record for observing more species of birds in one year that anyone else. He went on to attend college at the University of Arizona where he continued his birding expeditions. Parker had quite of skill when it came to identification, and quickly was deemed one of the best ornithologists around.

It's said that Parker had his own method when it came to birding that allowed him to expand his knowledge in both details and behavior. He was very generous with his knowledge and findings and regularly shared them with the birding community. Parker was killed in a plane crash in 1993 while in Ecuador. He was truly a marvel to the birding community that contributed greatly to the growth and knowledge of birding and identification.

Without the skill, knowledge, and contributions of these individuals, the birding community might not be where it is today. It's through the works of these people, as well as every other contributor in the birding community that has allowed the knowledge to grow in such massive proportions to where it is today.

One of the best ways for you to begin birding is to find other enthusiasts that can help you along as you start out. Birders are almost always willing to help you out and share their knowledge and tricks of the trade. It's very likely that there a local chapter in your area. If you don't find one through the Audubon Society you can also try local bird clubs or nature centers or visit birding.com to see if there are any organizations in your area.

The National Audubon Society

The National Audubon Society is a non-profit organization whose mission is to "conserve and restore natural ecosystems, focusing on birds, other wildlife, and their habitats for the benefit of humanity and the earth's biological diversity." The Audubon Society is over 100 years old with its origins dating to the 1900's being one of the oldest organizations of the kind. The Audubon Society has not only helped preserve many habitats, but has also been a guiding influence in legislation throughout the years.

Many acts have been brought to the attention of legislation as well as passed due to the influence of the Audubon Society. In 1918 the Migratory Bird Treaty act was passed by President Wilson which put in place the protection of migratory birds. In 1964 President Lyndon Johnson passed the Wilderness Act that set aside 9 million acres of protected wilderness. This was a major factor to protect wildlife habitats from the increasing population that threatened such areas. In 1973 the Endangered Species Act was passed by President Nixon. The Endangered Species Act allowed for the conservation of species on the brink of extinction. All these acts passed were a telling of the efforts put forth by the Audubon Society. Without their continuous determination throughout the last 100 years, many of the species we enjoy today would have tragically disappeared from the earth.

Preservation of animal habitats is not an easy task to accomplish, especially with the ever growing population and destruction of many natural habitats around the world. The Audubon Society recognized the need to rally their efforts into the protection of all animal species. In 1947 the Everglades National Park was established encompassing thousands of miles in the central Florida area. Protecting the Everglades has been a continuous battle for the Audubon. In 1974 the Lillian Annette Rowe Bird Sanctuary was opened in south central Nebraska becoming a home to many migratory birds such as the beautiful Whooping Crane. This sanctuary is actually owned and operated by the National Audubon Society. These are just a few of the victories of the Audubon in establishing habitats for our wildlife to continue on and prosper in; they continue in their fight for wildlife daily.

The American Birding Association

The American Biding Association (ABA) was formally known as the American Bird Watchers Association until 1969 when the name was

Bird Watching Mastery: What You Need To Know About Birds
changed to what it is today. The American Birding Association was a key element in the sport of birding and presenting it to the public. Before the ABA was formed in 1968 there were no formal publications on birding. Enthusiasts had to rely heavily on references from friends. It was extremely difficult to gain any information that would help in the process of identifying species as well as locating them.

Publications put out by the Audubon were mainly focused on conservation and little to do with bird identification. This all changed when the ABA was formed with the publication of the "Bird Watchers Digest" which was quickly changed to "Birding". It was through this publication that the guidelines for the ABA were discussed and agreed upon by avid birders. It was agreed upon that the main focus of the ABA would be the hobby and sport of birding. After about twenty years of this focus, it was finally agreed that the ABA would allow the topic of conservation to be addressed in addition to its primary focus of birding.

In the early years of the ABA, the "Birding" publication was the whole of the organization. Now with the passing of 39 years, the ABA has grown to encompass a wide range of communications in the birding community. With a ABA membership you are entitled to publications, participation in conferences, conventions, travel related benefits, ABA tours, ability to purchase gear through ABA sales, and a change to get involved in the community; definitely a far cry from the early days of the ABA. The ABA is a great organization aimed at birding interests such as identification, listing, education, and conservation.

Association of Field Ornithologists

The Association of Field Ornithologist (AFO) was founded in 1922. The AFO is one of the leading societies of both professional and beginner ornithologists. They are committed to the scientific study as well as the circulation of their studies about birds in their natural habitats. The AFO is a membership organization devoted to bird conservation and study. The AFO is a great source of communication between the beginner and professional ornithologist.

For those not familiar with the term ornithologist, it is basically someone who studies all aspects of birds. They focus on how they live, feed, evolve, the biology of a bird, and how they are affected by the changes in environment. The AFO is one of the six major societies in North America. Upon becoming a member you are provided with the quarterly "Journal of Field Ornithology", AFO association newsletter, invite the AFO annual meeting, discounts, and a bimonthly newsletter. A very informative tool when one has an interest in the inner workings of birds.

Chapter 7 - Important Behavior Observation During Bird Watching

What etiquette or ethics code needs to be followed in birding? As with any other sport or hobby there is a proper etiquette when it comes to birding for the beginner and novice alike. Each society has their publications on etiquette while birding. So what exactly does this mean for you? It means that it's important to familiarize yourself with the proper etiquette with any sport or hobby you are looking to pursue, preferably before you do it. Ignorance isn't a good excuse when there is plenty of literature to inform people, even those just starting out their birding experience.

The Rights of the Bird

As far as the birds themselves are concerned, they have rights too, just as people do. It's important for you to aid in the safety and wellbeing of birds and their environment. You wouldn't want someone coming into your house and trashing it, the same goes for birds while observing them. All animals are astute and can sense a human's presence. Try not to agitate them while birding and don't put them at risk. This means that it might not be wise to take too many pictures if photographing and that it's not always the right time to use recordings.

It has to be reiterated that endangered species are a major concern throughout the world. That being stated, it's important not to use any other methods than observation with any species that is endangered, of special concern, or is considered rare. It's extremely important not to do anything to disturb such species that are already experiencing such issues. Also, keep your enthusiasm at bay while birding and do not disturb nests. Birding is the act of observing birds in their natural habitat, not touching or taking.

So you're out birding and had the good fortune to find a rare bird species. Although you are probably ready to shout it from the highest tree and inform every organization and society you can think of, there are other factors to consider before doing so. First take into consideration how the bird will be affected as well as their habitat. If you advertise the bird's location will the bird be at risk? Also, where exactly is the bird located? If you are on your Uncle Earl's farm, consider that he might not want tons of people trespassing on their land to see a bird. It's definitely exciting be the one to experience a rare find, but remember that one of the main focuses of birding is the welfare of the birds.

Laws and Rights of Others

When birding, it's important to consider the laws of where you are as well as respecting the rights of other people. It is not ok to trespass on somebody's property. This is a clear violation of someone else's rights, and can be a danger to you. If you happen to spot a bird that you wish to observe on someone's property, stop and ask if you can go on their property. Chances are that the owner will give you the ok if they have an understanding of what you are doing and wish to accomplish.

Become familiar with any pertinent laws in the area you are planning to go birding in. Every state and area has different laws; it's wise to educate yourself beforehand. There might be certain areas that the public cannot go, even to observe birds. It might be the case that the area you plan to explore is a protected habitat. There might be certain areas that don't allow vehicles. It's worth the time of doing a little research to avoid any penalties that might occur if you break any laws, rules, or regulations. Officials won't be impressed or swayed with the phrase "I didn't know".

Creating your own Habitat

Many birding enthusiast create a bird friendly environment in their own backyard so they may experience the pleasure of birding without going far. There are many things to consider when doing this. When you place a bird feeder or other structure it is very important to keep it clean. This is also true for any water of food you place in the structure. If you don't pay attention you might just be offering rotten food or water that should not be consumed.

If you plan on setting up a structure to bring birds to your area, you need to make sure that it safe before doing so. If you own a dog or cat and keep it in the same area that you plan to set up the structure or habitat, you may need to rethink your strategy. You don't want to create a habitat in a potentially dangerous area. The same consideration needs to be followed if there are any hazardous materials in the proposed area. It's important to keep the welfare of the bird in mind at all times.

Michael Miller

When Birding in Groups

There is a difference when birding in solitude and when birding with a group. There are new things that the group needs to pay attention to. Everyone has to adhere to the basic etiquette in birding mentioned above. When going as a group you now have to consider those around you and not interfere with their birding experience. It's ok to share your information with others, it's actually preferred, especially to those that are just starting out.

Unfortunately there might be instances where you see a fellow birder doing something that they should not. If the behavior is something that you know should not be done it might be upon your shoulders to get involved if it's necessary. If it comes to this, do so in a friendly manner if possible. Let the individual doing wrong know exactly why their actions are unsuitable and ask for them to stop it. If the individual chooses to ignore your warning, then take note of it and any additional information needed so you can inform the proper individuals.

It's important to be a good example, not only to your fellow birders, but also to those outside the birding community. It's likely that other birders, especially beginners will take notice or your example and strive to follow. It's important to follow what you teach, don't say one thing, and then do another. Be responsible and make sure the group size is reasonable. You don't want a horde of people tramping through a bird's habitat. It's also important to remember that other people outside your birding group may be out enjoying nature or some other sport, be respectful of others.

Even if you are the leader of the group, it's important to make sure that everyone is aware of what they are supposed to be doing as well as not doing. Anyone in the group should share any useful

Bird Watching Mastery: What You Need To Know About Birds information about the area in which you are birding, especially if there are any no, no's. If you plan to go on a birding tour take heed that your tour guide knows what they are doing. It's their responsibility to make sure that birds come first. In all, have fun and enjoy your birding experience no matter where it is or who you go with. Just make sure to use the proper etiquette when doing so, this is so that everyone benefits, humans and birds alike.

Chapter 8- The Effects of Bird Watching to the Environment

Due to the growing interest in birding throughout the last documented 100 years there has been an increase in caring for the environment. Bird enthusiasts began observing birds in their natural habitats. In the process they were also able to observe the effects that development and growth had on the environment. It was through this distress that organizations such as that of the National Audubon Society were formed. It became their goal to fight for the habitats of birds and other animals in effort to preserve our environment.

Because of conservation efforts and birding enthusiasts laws were passed to protect species that would have otherwise gone extinct. The Migratory Bird Treaty Act was a major win in 1918 to keep bird wild American birds safe. The endangered species act was passed in 1973 in hopes of keeping wildlife such as the bald eagle from dying out of existence. Multiple land acts have been passed in order to set aside land for wildlife. These organizations have aided in the fight to clean up the air in order to fight global warming. They brought to attention the need to preserve or natural elements such as water.

Birding organizations have fought endlessly to preserve many natural habitats around the world. The Everglades National Park is a well known habitat that was almost completely destroyed by population growth and development. Through the efforts of many organizations it was able to be saved, in turn sparing all birds and other animals that find their home there that would have simply died out. Conservation efforts have saved habitats such as this all over, in turn saving thousands of species, not only animal, but plant, insect, fish, and many others.

Without the help of many birding organization as well as other animal organizations, the world would not be what it is today. Our environment would be vastly different. Many animals, plants, fish, and insects would most likely not exist. They would only be something to read about in books, or something that older generations merely remembered. Birding has had a very positive impact on the environment. Those in the birding community continuously contribute their information and knowledge to each other. Organizations found in birding as well as other nature groups strive to improve our environments for the sake of the animal factor as well as the human factor, we are all connected.

Backyard Birding

Many birding enthusiasts love to watch birds where ever they are. For this reason, many turn their backyards into a bird haven. This is fairly easy for anyone to do and provides the pleasure of looking out your back window and spotting an array of birds without having to leave your house. There are several steps you can take to make your backyard a bird paradise. There are both short term and long term steps to be taken to accomplish this. There are also several factors to consider.

Food and Shelter

First you need to make sure that your backyard is a suitable place for birds to dwell. If you house your dogs or cats in your backyard then it might not be a bird friendly environment. You really don't want to come out one morning with the hopes of birding only to discover Rover covered with feathers. Also it's not fair to your existing pets to have birds zipping in and out of your backyard while expecting your pets not to take a swat at them; it's in their nature to do so and really not fair to penalize them for it. You need to make sure that it will be a safe environment for the birds before trying to attract them.

You can then start with a bird feeder or bird house. It's important to note that depending on the bird's preferences, different bird houses will attract different birds. Some birds may not adapt to bird houses. You can do some research to see what type of bird house to get. The location of the bird feeder or bird house is also critical, chose a place that is safe. Once you get a feeder or bird house up it time to fill it with some food to attract the birds. Again, the type of food you put out will attract different types of birds. You may choose to offer a variety of food to attract many kinds of birds.

Water

Now that you have the food covered, there are many options for providing water to you feathered friends. Many feeders have a place to put water. Another option is to install a bird bath, bird fountain, or some sort of pond. Birds aren't too picky; anything that they can access that retains shallow water will make them happy. You can choose something inexpensive or choose to add to the value of your backyard and put in something that might be a little more costly, but adds to the appeal of your home. Just remember to change out the water regularly if you choose a method that offers standing water. It's also important to clean feeders and watering areas to avoid the spread of diseases between birds.

Plants and Trees

Now that you have the easy tasks complete, it's time to think more long term. Take a good look around your backyard. Are there trees, shrubs, and flowers? If your backyard is pretty bare there are plenty of things you can do to attract birds that will keep them coming back. You need to provide them with an appealing habitat, plus you can make your backyard look great in the process. Plant a variety of small trees and bushes. There are many types that certain types that offer food and nesting opportunities to birds depending on where you live.

For those in the Northeast a great bush to consider is the Highbush Blueberry which is a shrub. This bush can draw up to as many as 30 different species of birds such as the Brown Thrasher and Gray Catbird. It's a pretty shrub that will eventually offer berries to the birds when it matures. It also provides them with great nesting opportunities. The Eastern Red Cedar is a great tree if you have a large backyard. This tree can grow up to 65 feet and is a great home for many birds like the Ruffed Grouse and Yellow-bellied Sapsucker. The Eastern Red Cedar provides nuts and can attract many species.

For those in the Southeast the Arrowwood Viburnum is a shrub that produces berries in the late summer months. It's an attractive plant that also offers great nesting sites to various birds such as the

Eastern Bluebird and American Robin. The Southern Magnolia is a beautiful tree that can grow as tall as 90 feet. It's a fruit producing tree that matures in the fall. The Southern Magnolia attracts different species such as that of the Red-bellied Woodpecker and the Northern Mockingbird.

For those in the Central Plains and Praries the Big Bluestem is a beautiful grass like plant that produces seeds as well as nesting opportunities for over 24 species of birds such as the Sedge Wren and Meadowlark. It's a plant that provides great cover and attracts many different song birds. The Gray Dogwood is a large shrub that can grow up to 9 feet. It provides fruit berries to birds such as the Northern Cardinal and Eastern Bluebird.

For those in Western Mountains and Deserts the Mesquite is a multi-stemmed shrub which can grow up to 15 feet and a single stemmed tree that can grow a tall as 40 feet. It provides seeds, cover, and nesting grounds to birds such as the Gambel's Quail and White-winged Dove. The Rocky Mountain Juniper can be considered either a shrub or a tree and can grow to 30 feet. It provides nutlets that offer birds such as the Northern Mockingbird and Evening Grosbeak great coverage.

For those in the Pacific Coast the California Wax Myrtle is a shrub or small tree that can reach 35 feet. It's a great source of food that produces fruit all year long, even during winter months. A bird to can benefit from this plant is the Yellow-rumped Warbler and California Towhee, amongst others. The California Wild Oak is a beautiful shrub-like tree that can reach 85 feet. You definitely need to make sure you have the room for this tree. It offers nuts and fruit to birds such as the Western Scrub Jay and Chestnut-backed Chickadee. It creates great coverage for the birds and is a very easy tree to maintain.

Bird Watching Mastery: What You Need To Know About Birds

Depending on your area, another option for trees are fruit trees. This way both you and the birds can benefit. Great trees to consider are lemon, apple, and cherry. They offer birds the sweet blossoms followed by fruit. The birds can get their food from the tree and you can have a freshly grown apple when you like. It's a winning combination for all and a great way to grow your own fruit.

Flowers are another great idea that will not only attract birds, but will make your yard look great. This is especially a good idea if you are interested in attracting humming birds. Humming birds love the sweet nectar that flowers provide. It's good to plant a variety such as sunflowers, marigolds, and poppies. You can even look into adding vine-like plants that will add to the ambiance of your yard as well as attract birds. In the end, you garden will be breathtaking. You need to make sure to be adding native plants that will survive in your area and those birds will be comfortable with.

National Wildlife Federation

Once you have created your bird paradise you have the option of Contacting the National Wildlife Federation. They encourage home owners to create wildlife gardens for birds and other animals. They recognize the importance of giving back to wildlife what progress and development have taken away. When you are done creating your backyard you can check to see if it matches the guidelines of the National Wildlife Federation. If it does then you can get a National Wildlife Federation display that shows your contribution to the environment.

After all that work you now have a backyard that will attract birds for many years to come. You just might wake up to the sounds of birds chirping happily in the morning hours. You can sit and watch the birds while you eat your breakfast or drink your coffee. You can enjoy all the aspects of birding while sitting in your pajamas. Life is now great for the birding enthusiast.

About The Author

Michael Miller is nationally known as bird artist and an author of many birding books. He has participated in many documentary films concerning bird watching. His passion and love for nature has drove Michael to participate and write different books about birds and nature and in return people will be more appreciative on the beauty of nature and on birds in particular.

Michael Miller is happily married and is blessed with four kids.

CPSIA information can be obtained
at www.ICGtesting.com
Printed in the USA
BVOW07s0625160217
476364BV00034B/11/P